by

Diana Burbano

(she/her/hers)

www.stagerights.com

GHOSTS OF BOGOTÁ

For all stage performance inquiries, please contact:

Steele Spring Stage Rights
3845 Cazador Street
Los Angeles, CA 90065
(323) 739-0413
www.stagerights.com

Artwork by Rob Dario, 2019.

Ghosts of Bogotá

ORIGINAL PRODUCTION CREDITS

Ghosts of Bogotá was written as a commission for AlterLab. It was developed over the course of the year with in-house developmental readings. It went on to win the NuVoices Festival at Actors Theatre of Charlotte and the Rella Lossy Award, both for 2019. The play was supported in part by a grant from the Arts Council for Long Beach and the City of Long Beach.

AlterTheater presents
Ghosts of Bogotá
by Diana Burbano

CAST
[in order of appearance]

Teresa .... Linda Girón
Sandy .... Carla Pauli
Lola .... Livia Gomes Demarchi*
Bruno .... Eduardo Soria
Nena .... Leticia Duarte
Saúl .... Tony Ortega
Jesus .... Noe Flores

PRODUCTION TEAM

Director .... Alicia Coombes
Dramaturg .... Jeanette Harrison
Stage Manager .... Christine L. Plowright
Sound Designer .... Gerry Grosz
Costume Designer .... Adriana Gutierrez
Fine Artist .... Stephanie Jucker
Props .... Christine L. Plowright

Artwork provided by Stephanie Jucker and Barbara Poole.

**Member of Actors' Equity Association. This theater operates under an agreement with Actors' Equity Association, the Union of Professional Actors and Stage Managers in the United States.*

Ghosts of Bogotá

CHARACTER DESCRIPTIONS

Minimum Casting Requirements:
3-4F (Tere and Nena can double), 2M, 1 Any Gender (Jesus)

LOLA: Eldest sibling. Dramatic, overbearing. Successful TV showrunner. Not into sympathy. (Late 30s, F)

SANDY: Middle sibling. No nonsense, practical, brutally honest, but has a very squishy center. (30s, F)

BRUNO: The baby. Hip. American-born. Likes his pleasures. (20s, M)

NENA: Their grandmother's ghost. Funny, bubbly. Doubles Teresa. (Any age, F)

TERESA: The young woman who cared for their dead grandfather. Smart. Manipulative. Speaks Spanish. (Late teens, F)

JESUS: A creepy Jesus head in a jar. A puppet, or a disembodied voice or??? (Any)

SAÚL: Their grandfather's ghost. Very, very charming. (Any age, M)

CHARACTERS & SETTING

The play takes place in Bogotá, Colombia as seen through the eyes of three uber-Americanized Colombian siblings. Sandy is pretty bilingual, Lola less so. Nena, Saúl, and Tere should be played by bilingual actors.

All the actors are Latinx. Jesus if he is cast as a human should be Afro-Latinx, or Black.

PLACE

An apartment, a cathedral, Monserraté. Bogotá, Colombia.

TIME

Now.

RUN TIME

90 minutes

Ghosts of Bogotá

GENERAL NOTES

Please. Do not use the word TELENOVELA to refer to anything or anyone while rehearsing, producing, or reviewing this play. There are many, many, many other ways to talk about Latinx work.

For pre- and post-show music: Please consider Rockera's En Español, and not stuff like Pollera Colorá: https://open.spotify.com/playlist/0RpTPZ9E8ylqhmHg9oiWvH?si=1ZBTzjDnTI6QISTH8BTVCg

“Chao” is the Colombian spelling of “ciao.”

Epigenetics: The study of changes in organisms caused by modification of gene expression rather than alteration of the genetic code itself. http://www.bbc.com/future/story/20190326-whatis-epigenetics

Juan Valdez Café https://www.juanvaldezcafe.com/en-us/

Usaquén is a trendy neighborhood in Bogotá.

The Candelaria is a historic neighborhood in the Bogotá's downtown.

The TransMilenio is Bogotá's not so rapid transit system.

Monserrate is a hill that dominates the city center of Bogotá. It has a 17th century church with a shrine, devoted to El Señor Caído ("The Fallen Lord").

Rio Magdalena is the principal river of Colombia. It takes its name from the biblical figure Mary Magdalene.

Yes, the Creepy Jesus head is real. See picture at the end of script.

"Colorin colora'o este cuento se acaba'o." is how Disney ended their children's records. It rhymes. The word is "Acabado" but w/o the D.

PERFORMANCE NOTES

Before the show please acknowledge the Native Peoples upon whose land the play is being performed.

A \ means the dialogue should fly.

Ghosts of Bogotá

AUTHOR'S NOTE

I've worked in the theater as an actor since I was 12 years old.

I played my first Latinx character when I was 23.

Work was always tough to find as an adult, and I spent a lot of years doubting myself, my skill, wondering why I had so many great callbacks, but never ultimately found the parts that were meaningful and felt "In the pocket." I stopped acting after one too many times being faced with, "But what are you?" Or, "You're great, but just not-quite-right." "If we produce it in Spanish—!"

I started writing. I wanted to write something for myself to perform, but soon it became clear that what I was really doing was writing myself and others like me back into the story.

Female, Latinx, intelligent, flawed, interesting, messy, ridiculous. All these things I had not had a chance to portray as an actor because the parts didn't exist or weren't being produced.

Thanks to AlterTheater for taking a chance on my need to examine my life onstage and to Stage Rights for publishing the result. For the first time in my stage life, I feel seen, in wholeness. And it's messy and joyful and dark and complicated and human. Imperfect, but in a truthful way. Laughing through pain.

To have my play produced is wonderful, but my greatest joy is that my plays seem to resonate deeply for performers. Especially women. Especially Latinx women. I'm so happy to have roles for women to play that don't hinge on any stereotypes but are very much about the experience of being a woman of Latinx heritage living in America.

We are at the beginning of a movement. Latinx work is becoming an important part of the larger theatrical conversation. There is beauty in Latinx plays, and everyone is unique and new and very personal to the playwright. We speak only for ourselves.

I'm not part of a monolith.

I'm excited to share this story with the theatre community. Is it universal? I think everyone will see something of themselves in it. In its specificity to my experience, I think many others will find resonance too.

PROLOGUE: UNKNOWN JUNGLES

The sound of a tropical jungle, birds, monkeys, frogs. It is lush and soothing, wild and beautiful. The sound fills the void until:

FLIGHT ATTENDANT (V.O.): Buenas noches. Por favor, ajusten sus sillas y mesas. El tiempo es 23:22. Bienvenidos a Bogotá.

The jungle sound becomes the crackle of an airplane landing.

SCENE SHIFT:

CASAS DESCONOCIDAS

The stage is dark. A door opens, and a light clicks on. It is a small apartment in Bogotá, filled to the brim with objects and neglected looking.

TERESA (O.S.): Pasen, por favor. Estan en su casa! Su abuelo hablaba de ustedes todito el tiempo. Que pena que no vinieron antes de qu'el falleció.

TERESA enters. She is a cute young woman, dressed in tight jeans and a low-cut blouse. She is followed by LOLA, in tired-looking but hip athleisure wear and an Hermés Birkin purse; SANDY, the younger sister, tightly wound; and baby brother BRUNO. They are all Colombians but have lived in America so long, they seem like gringos.

BRUNO: What did she say?

SANDY: Oh my god. Have you forgotten everything?

She speaks Spanish with a Spanish-from-Spain accent.

Gracias, Teresa, pero con el trabajo es difícil venir a Colombia.

TERESA: Eh— cómo?

SANDY: Ah, disculpe, aprendí mi español en España.

LOLA *(as if sneezing)*: Pretentious!

In Spanish to Teresa. Lola has an American accent, but speaks Spanish fairly well.

Y más, yo lo odiaba, so pa' que torturarme?

SANDY: Lola, shut up.

LOLA: Don't tell me—

TERESA: Sí. Tan Americanos! I practice English, I watch your TV show!

BRUNO: Right on, "Booster rockets, go!"

TERESA: Uh... sí!!

She and BRUNO make the same cheesy gesture.

LOLA: God. That wasn't my idea. The idiot actor improvised that and it became a catchphrase.

TERESA *(at a loss)*: Ok. No sé?

BRUNO: And a meme!

LOLA: And tee-shirts, lunchboxes, sexy costumes. And I get the money, not him!

LOLA & BRUNO: "Booster Rockets, go!"

LOLA and BRUNO make the same cheesy gesture, much to SANDY's annoyance.

SANDY: Can both of you just shut up?

BRUNO *(under his breath)*: Fuck off.

SANDY: Gracias Teresa, estamos requéte cansados. Con permiso?

BRUNO: Ask her if there is any beer?

LOLA: You ask her.

BRUNO: I'll go out later, ask her what's the wifi?

TERESA: No hay internet. No sirve!

BRUNO: What! Shit, I have to work!

TERESA: Hay un café internet en la esquina.

SANDY: There's a cafe on the corner.

BRUNO *(bad accent)*: Cerveza?

TERESA *(flirty)*: Te puedo mostrar.

BRUNO *(flirty right back)*: Ooookay!? Cool. I think?

(To Lola)

I need to tell Hamid where I am. I'll get a new card for my phone tomorrow.

SANDY: We are arranging a funeral tomorrow.

BRUNO: It won't take all day!

LOLA: There are days I really regret I quit drinking.

(To Bruno)

Go.

He exits.

(To Teresa)

Tienes otra llave?

TERESA: Sólo ésta.

She hands LOLA an old-fashioned key.

LOLA: Nice. It's all like House of the Spirits and shit.

TERESA looks at LOLA and SANDY.

TERESA: Él siempre hablaba de ustedes. Que bonitas eran de chiquitas. "Las Rolas." Que pena que nunca lo vinieron a ver!

SANDY: Sí. Una tristeza. Gracias, Teresa, nos vemos mañana, vale?

TERESA: Ah, pues, sí. Si necesitan cualquier cosa me llaman?

SANDY: Claro.

LOLA: Hey, how did he die?

SANDY shoots her a dirty look.

SANDY: Stop it. Chao, Teresa.

TERESA: Chao, niñas, que duermen.

She exits. LOLA and SANDY stand in the middle of the unfamiliar apartment and look around.

SANDY: What a mess.

LOLA *(dismissive)*: Niñas. I'm old enough to be her— incredibly attractive older sister. Bleah. Everything smells like bread and mold. I'm exhausted. Where are we supposed to sleep?

They both look to the bedrooms.

Fuck no. I'm not sleeping in the dead man's bed. Bruno will do it, he won't care.

SANDY: Ha. That's what he gets for leaving. He's such an asshole. I don't think he's said two sentences to me this whole trip.

LOLA: Yah. You're both way fun to be around.

SANDY: Can you talk to him—

LOLA: Nope. No, I will not. I'm not even sure what time-zone I'm in.

SANDY: Three hours earlier than LA.

LOLA: What time is that?

SANDY: Right, your fake dyslexia.

LOLA: It's not fake!

SANDY: Stop performing. You're not on Late Night. It's 1:54 a.m., we have to be up and out at 7.

LOLA: FUUUCK me. Who makes appointments that early?

SANDY: Catholic priests.

LOLA: Fine. I'll take the couch.

Goes rummaging for blankets.

SANDY: I'll sleep in the maid's room.

LOLA *(under her breath)*: Appropriate.

SANDY: What?

LOLA: Nada— Ugh, these blankets look like they were originally covered in smallpox! They're barely holding together!

She holds up a few ratty woolen blankets.

SANDY: I packed my down comforter.

LOLA: Dude. What about me?

SANDY: I didn't pack you one.

LOLA *(whining)*: I'm freeeeeezing!!

SANDY: Goodnight. I'll shower first in the morning.

LOLA: Fine. Brrr. This place sucks.

SANDY: I know.

LOLA: Can we move into a hotel tomorrow?

SANDY: You can. I spent my savings on the plane ticket. Goodnight.

Exits.

LOLA *(yelling after her)*: You're a doctor! How are you so poor? Oh my god! It is so cold!!

LOLA opens her case, and considers taking out her PJ's. She decides to sleep in her track suit and just takes off her shoes. The floor is tile, and freezing. She wedges herself on the small sofa, realizes she has to turn off the light and goes to hunt for the switch. She turns it off but the room is lit up by a powerful streetlight outside the window. She tries to sleep when a passing car illuminates an object in a glass case. Lola screams. SANDY runs in with her pajamas on and her toothbrush in her mouth.

Oh my god. What is that thing?

She points to the thing in the case. It is a disembodied head, quite dead and blue and very gruesome.

SANDY: Ew.

LOLA: Jesus. Oh, it IS Jesus.

SANDY: No it can't be—

LOLA: —Yeah, look, he's got a crown of thorns. Oh wow, that is— demented.

SANDY: Creepy Jesus!

LOLA: Creepy Jesus head in a jar. It looks real.

SANDY: Imagine having that thing staring at you while you are eating.

LOLA: Or fucking. It is the most hideous thing I've ever seen.

SANDY: Well, cover it.

LOLA: Help me find something.

They search around. SANDY goes in the bathroom and finds a toilet paper cozy with a doll torso on top. She tries that. It fits, but the chin is still seen underneath.

"Hi, I'm Creepy Jesus, and I died for your sins!" "Hee, hee, sit on your face Creepy Jesus."

SANDY *(laughing)*: You are such an idiot.

LOLA continues her puppet show.

LOLA: Get under my skirts creepy Jesus!

SANDY: Ok. Stop. Go to bed.

LOLA: I can't sleep.

SANDY: You haven't even tried.

LOLA flops onto the couch, dust flies out.

LOLA: UUUGGGGHHH! I hate it here.

SANDY: Well, if you and Bruno had decided you wanted to come when we found out Saúl was on his last legs, instead of this morning, Tia Reyna might have been able to find a place for us that wasn't— this.

LOLA: This is extra rotten bad karma. I feel like we need to burn sage.

SANDY: Or whatever Colombians do to clear out spaces.

LOLA: Yeah... I don't know... Sit on grapes?

SANDY: That's for luck on New Year's Eve. I think... I'm going to bed. Are you OK?

LOLA: No. I don't know why I came. I hated him.

SANDY: Ok.

LOLA: You hated him too.

SANDY: You don't know what I feel.

LOLA: C'mon. He abused us both.

SANDY: Let's not talk about this right now. Please.

LOLA: I can feel him in here. He's asking for forgiveness.

SANDY: Calm down your crazy. I just spent nine hideous hours on the plane being ignored by Bruno. My patience is at, like, nil.

LOLA: I don't want to calm down. I want to take a sledgehammer to all his stuff. I want to scream at all our women relatives who let him get away with everything. I want to cut off his balls.

SANDY: He's dead.

LOLA: I want a trophy.

SANDY: Take Creepy Jesus. He'd be great company.

LOLA: Maybe I will.

She sighs.

It's weird to be here, without mom, without Nena. They would've danced on his corpse.

SANDY: You're projecting.

LOLA: I feel sick. I wish we had a hotel. I can feel his weight on me now.

SANDY: Do you want to come sleep with me?

LOLA: Ew. No, that's weird.

SANDY: You're freaked out and I have a down comforter.

LOLA: Oh.

LOLA turns to go into the bedroom, then turn back.

LOLA (CONT'D) *(seriously)*: Sandy. Do you believe in Epigenetics?

SANDY: Yes, and Santa Claus.

LOLA: I'm serious. All that conquistador trauma— I've been reading how it lives on in our bodies.

SANDY: Where do you get your info, Facebook? Go, put yourself to bed.

LOLA exits. SANDY goes to the Creepy Jesus and takes the doll off him. She puts it back on like a jaunty hat. She smiles a cat smile, and exits into the bedroom.

LIGHTS OUT.

DREAMS

NENA, who could be a young girl or an old woman, comes in and pulls a book out from under the couch cushion. She opens it. It is full of paper dolls, cut from magazines. She plays with them.

NENA *(in a sing-song, a children's nursery rhyme)*: La india más linda se fue al rey!

La segunda india, al capitán!

La tercera, de piel oscura y muy fea,

Se la dieron al sacer-do-o-te.

Full stop. The next spoken very rapidly:

Conquien tuvo siete hijas, cada una más fea que la anterior.

LIGHTS OUT.

TALK TALK

Light streams into the apartment. The noise from outside is intense. SANDY enters, dressed very practically, drip dry and wearing good walking shoes. She sees something on the floor, frowns and looks for a broom. LOLA enters. She has eccentric, expensive taste. She wears high boots.

LOLA *(barely awake)*: Coffee. Coffee.

SANDY: Go make it.

LOLA *(rummaging sleepily around the kitchen)*: No machine. Where machine?

SANDY: They drink Nescafé here.

LOLA *(awake; in shock)*: Wait. Wut?

SANDY *(making a face)*: I know. We can go to Juan Valdez after the meeting.

LOLA: The donkey dude?

SANDY: It's like Starbucks.

LOLA: But now?

SANDY: Nescafé.

LOLA makes a pleading face.

(Unrelenting)

Boil the water.

LOLA makes a bigger pleading face.

(UGH)

Never mind, I'll do it. Go wake Bruno up.

LOLA: He'll murder me. I'll text him.

Grabs her phone.

Shit, it doesn't work, fucking AT&T. Where is he?

SANDY points to the main bedroom. LOLA grimaces, takes off her boot and throws it at the door. Does it with the other one. Retrieves them and does it again.

SANDY: Can you just go in and wake him up?

LOLA: No. He punches!

At that moment, BRUNO comes in the front door, carrying Juan Valdez coffees in a cardboard tray.

Oh my god, you have saved me. I am saved.

BRUNO: Here, this one has oat milk.

LOLA: They do oat milk here?

BRUNO:
It's 2020! Where have you been?

SANDY:
Hello dipshit, what do you think avena is?

BRUNO: Are you ready?

LOLA: Did you ever go to bed?

BRUNO: Sleep is for losers. Found a strip club where they paint the chicks in UV and they dance under blacklight. They had Wifi. Got a lot of work done.

SANDY *(to Lola)*: Oh my fuck.

BRUNO *(to Lola)*: They were pretty grateful for the American cash.

(With pleasure)

Big thighed women on poles. HMMMM.

SANDY *(to Lola)*: Supporting sex slavery and exploitation—

BRUNO: It's a local economy.

SANDY *(spluttering)*: Men like you—!

LOLA: Can you guys hold those thoughts? You can snipe each other to death after I'm caffeinated.

LOLA puts on her boots. BRUNO puts the tray of coffees down. SANDY eyes him.

SANDY *(icily)*: Thank you.

BRUNO *(equally icy)*: You're welcome.

(To Lola)

Where exactly are we going?

SANDY *(to Lola)*: Iglesia San Agustín.

BRUNO checks on his phone.

BRUNO: We are in Usaquén, and that is in the Candelaria. According to Waze, It's going to take us an hour and a half.

SANDY: It's only two miles away!

BRUNO: Bogotá traffic is legendary, OK? The Lonely Planet rates it "Impossible to get around."

SANDY *(pulling out a mess of tourist maps)*: Let's take the TransMilenio.

LOLA: Here! Are you nuts?

SANDY: Don't be such a Caucasian.

LOLA: When we get kidnapped I'm not giving the drug lords my Hermès Birkin.

SANDY: Do you know how many kids I could immunize for what that bag cost?

LOLA: Excuse me, Saint Sandra of the Slums. I gave your foundation a huge donation, don't make me feel guilty for having money.

BRUNO *(checking his pockets)*: Do they take Venmo? I gave all my cash to the strippers.

SANDY *(eye roll)*: I have cash. Let's go.

The doorbell rings. BRUNO goes to open it. LOLA, in an irrational panic, stops him.

LOLA: Wait! They throw acid at peoples faces around here!

Both BRUNO and SANDY look at LOLA like she's finally lost it.

It's something men do around here! To get revenge on women! I swear!

SANDY *(drily)*: You lived with a method actor who had a collection of firearms and you're worried about getting killed here?

BRUNO *(forgetting he's not talking to Sandy)*: OOH. That dude was all mild and midwestern, like a serial killer. Creeeeepy.

LOLA *(dismissive)*: Those guns were fake. He collected them for his cheap-o storefront theatre shows. So they would cast him. God. Actors are gross.

Doorbell rings. LOLA jumps. SANDY looks out the window.

SANDY: It's our cousin Carlos.

(Yelling)

Hola, Carlos!

CARLOS (O.S.) *(a VERY young male voice)*: Tengo el carro! Vamos!

SANDY: Oh, great. He'll drive us.

LOLA: Isn't he 12?

SANDY: Let's go. Key?

They look at LOLA. She starts looking for it. BRUNO exits. SANDY rolls her eyes, exits after him. Lola scurries around looking for her purse, her phone and a lipstick, and the key, which she has scattered all over the room. She drops something, looks under the couch, pulls out a mass of paper dolls.

LOLA: What the–?

SANDY (O.S.): Lola! Hurry up!

LOLA stuffs the dolls in her purse.

LIGHTS OUT.

LA OTRA

SANDY and LOLA are sitting uncomfortably on the couch. TERESA is crying. They have a huge tray of béchamel lasagna in front of them and two empty plates.

TERESA *(continuing a long, appalling story)*: ...Y se murió así! Encima de mí! Casi me sofocó.

LOLA: There is no fucking justice!

TERESA *(crying)*: Ahora dónde vamos a vivir!! Pobrecita mi hijita!

SANDY: Hijta?

TERESA: Sí— de tu abuelo.

(Sniffle)

Que escándalo.

LOLA: Escándalo? It's gross that's what it is. How old are you?

SANDY: Shut up! Teresa, mira, yo no quiero la pension, tampoco queremos este apartamento.

LOLA: Don't give her the fucking apartment!

SANDY: We don't need it!

LOLA: It should have been Nena's! Not some immoral bitch who fucked him for his pension!! Shit, she'll go after my money next.

TERESA: Sí, money. Un little money, hasta que puedo encontrar empleo.

LOLA: Please tell me you murdered him on purpose!

SANDY: LOLA! Teresa, yo de verdad no sé que hacer. Es un tangulo.

LOLA: Tangulo? That's not a real word.

SANDY: Que podemos hacer? No eres esposa, verdad?

LOLA: Of course she's not his fucking wife!

SANDY: He was a widower, stupid! It's possible.

TERESA: El viejo me dejó sin nada.

SANDY: De veras no se que hacer.

LOLA *(very, VERY bad Spanish)*: You said that already. Look. Mira. Hablamos más cuando acabamos con el funeralio. Pero, ahora necesitamos—

Stuck for the word, she makes an over-the-top burying gesture.

—bury him in the ground.

TERESA: Pero no puedes enterrarlo! No ves? Se murió sin hacer su confesion.

LOLA: Confession? So they won't bury him? That's— medieval.

SANDY: They buy into that whole sin thing.

LOLA: Yeah, but he paid out the ass for a niche!

TERESA: Sí! Siempre dió mucha money a la iglesia. Para no ir—

TERESA gestures down as if pointing to hell.

LOLA: Bueno, porque no le haces un woo-woo de magia?

SANDY: Um, what?

LOLA: If she's worried he's going to go to hell, can't she do some kind of Latin American voodoo or something?

SANDY: The voodoo here is called Catholicism.

TERESA: No sé que hacer. ¡Ayúdenme, plis!

LOLA: Comó se dice— you made your damn bed.

TERESA stops crying and changes tack. She takes a tin cookie box out of her purse, and shoves it toward LOLA.

TERESA: Tome. No quiero que me vaya a embrujar.

LOLA *(reaching eagerly for a cookie)*: Oh, I love these.

She goes to open it.

TERESA: No! Ahí están las cenizas.

LOLA: Cenizas?

SANDY: Ashes, you dingbat—

LOLA: Oh. Oh! Ewwww.

SANDY: Teresa—

LOLA: —We're still not giving you this apartamento.

SANDY: Todas estamos cansadas. Mañana hablamos, OK?

TERESA: Sí. Sé que me van a ayudar. Sé que son unas mujercitas buenas y Cristianas.

LOLA and SANDY look at each other and burst out laughing. Sandy gathers herself and escorts TERESA out the door. Lola stares at the cookie tin. Nudges it further away from her with her foot.

SANDY *(still laughing)*: My god. You're an epic pain.

LOLA: Christianas my fat ass!

SANDY: Lola, he clearly victimized her. And there's a kid.

LOLA: Forget it. She's a ho.

SANDY: You'll save a dozen ugly dogs, but you haven't got one ounce of compassion for a woman, who, frankly, saved us from having to deal with a man we hated while he died.

LOLA: We don't owe her or him anything.

SANDY gets up wearily.

SANDY: I'm going to the mercado.

LOLA *(whiny)*: No! Don't leave me here with him. It. This!

Indicating the cookie tin, the Jesus head, the apartment.

SANDY: I need Alka-Seltzer and a huge bottle of the local red.

LOLA *(longingly)*: Oooh, a bottle of wine sounds so good right now.

SANDY *(on alert)*: I'm sorry. Is that a problem?

LOLA: Go ahead. Us drunks don't like to be bummers.

SANDY: I don't want to make you fall off the wagon.

LOLA: I know this is hard to believe, but I can control myself.

SANDY: Do you need to go to a meeting?

LOLA *(dismissive)*: Do they even have AA here?

SANDY: Yes. I checked there's a meeting in Siete de Agosto—

LOLA *(cutting her off)*: You— checked?

SANDY: Just in case.

LOLA: I don't do AA. I used a hypnotist.

SANDY: What?

LOLA: AA is full of assholes that believe in god.

(At Sandy's disbelief)

It's only got like a 10% success rate. Very loserish.

SANDY: Why do you think you are better than everyone else?

LOLA: Just go. Can you bring me some pan de yucca?

SANDY: How can you eat? I'll never be able to look at food ever again. I'll bet there was heavy cream in that.

(Points at lasagna)

I'd better get Lactaid, or it'll be toot city around here.

LOLA: I can't believe you ate her food. She probably tried to poison us.

SANDY: Leave the rest for Bruno.

LOLA: Bruno doesn't eat white food. Hey— That priest this morning, he was flirting with me, right?

SANDY: Yes. I think he was.

LOLA: That's weird, right?

SANDY: I mean— I suppose you are marginally, famous-ish. Doesn't that happen to you all the time?

LOLA *(sighs)*: Dude, why couldn't that priest be hot?

SANDY: I don't think there has ever been a truly hot priest.

LOLA: I dunno. That whole cassock thing is pretty fucking sexy.

SANDY: Padre Arévalo looks like a black cupcake in that thing.

LOLA: Nomnomnom

SANDY *(gross)*: I'm going to go before it gets dark and I get shivved walking back.

LOLA *(mutters)*: We should be so lucky.

SANDY: Jerk. Try and find the heater while I'm gone. Where's the key?

LOLA: God. I dunno. It totally disappeared! I'll look for another set of keys.

SANDY *(looks around)*: I guess we should start figuring out how we are going to get rid of this stuff— I don't want to dig through these piles. Maybe we should give Teresa the apartment.

LOLA: No way. Just go. And get back quickly please.

SANDY exits out the front door. LOLA waits. When she's sure Sandy is gone, she takes out a small bottle of Aguardiente. She hears a noise and hides the Aguardiente under the couch cushion. NENA comes out crying; she starts when she sees Lola.

Nena?

NENA: Now you come? I hope you're pleased with yourself!

NENA hears a noise behind her and starts to run. SAÚL, an old man, enters. He is drunk. He grabs Nena and drags her back where she came.

Not again!! Lola! Por favor!

A BLINDING FLASH OF LIGHT:

MODERN LOVE

LOLA sits on the couch, rubbing her aching head, she takes the Aguardiente bottle out, starts to open it. Bruno enters from the outside. He's a little high. He's carrying a bag of empanadas.

BRUNO: Yo.

LOLA: Tú qué?

BRUNO grabs the bottle of Aguardiente and drinks it.

BRUNO *(offering the bag)*: You want one?

LOLA *(massaging her temple)*: Ow. No. Yes. Cheese? Want some lasagna?

BRUNO: Hell, yes— Ew! Why is it white??

LOLA: It's bechamel. We got a panful from every relative we visited today. This was the third one.

BRUNO hands her an empanada. She starts to eat.

I— my head hurts.

BRUNO: It's the smog.

He finishes the little Aguardiente bottle. Places it next to the Creepy Jesus, seeing it for the first time.

Oh shit! What the fuck is that?

LOLA: He died for your sins, man. Have some respect.

BRUNO: Jesus. That's the goriest thing I've ever seen. So much for metaphor.

LOLA: Amen.

BRUNO: This thing would be amazing at my Halloween party.

LOLA: Good luck getting it through customs. You already look like a terrorist. They'll kill you before they figure out it's a statue.

BRUNO: Is it though? It's so realistic—

LOLA: Oh, my god. Don't go there.

BRUNO: Huh. Just saying. I'm not looking at that thing too closely.

LOLA: Thanks. I will literally never sleep again.

LOLA covers the Jesus head with the toilet paper doll.

Bruno. Speak to Sandy. I'm so done.

BRUNO: No.

LOLA: C'mon.

BRUNO: She's never apologized.

LOLA: She never will!

BRUNO: Do you know what a buzzkill it is to get a box full of condoms and pamphlets about venereal disease?

LOLA: You had to tell her you were pansexual.

BRUNO: I was trying to share my life!

LOLA: Pansexuality is not everyone's bag, baby. Especially an epidemiologist.

BRUNO: She's judgey as fuck.

LOLA: Well I'm not judgey, I'm grateful. The weirder your life is, the better my scripts are.

BRUNO: Why don't I get royalties?

LOLA: It's ALL yours when I die.

BRUNO: You and the Sand Crab are so different. You're cool, and she's— shit. I don't know.

LOLA: You gotta give her a break. She's a little clam. I never knew she went through the same shit I did until she came home from her first year of grad school. I was driving her and her anorexic girlfriend to the airport, remember her?

BRUNO: Carrie?

LOLA: Cassie.

BRUNO: The one that died.

LOLA: Yeah, duh, she weighed like, 80 pounds. Poor Sand. Anyway, Sand had barely come out to me, and I had taken over the conversation, yammering, declaiming, talking about being molested by Saúl, you know, my typical grand overshare, and Cassie said, very bossily, "Sandy was abused too."

BRUNO: Whoa.

SANDY enters, listens without being seen.

LOLA: Yeah. That shut me up. Ha. I stopped the car hard. Looked at Sand. She's staring at the floor and says quietly, "I'm in therapy".

BRUNO tsks sympathetically.

The only thing that had been my saving grace was that it had just been me, and I was definitely a bad punkass bitch. I could take any shit life threw at me, but when I realized I hadn't protected her, my baby sister from this monster— How much more of a big fucking failure could I be?

BRUNO: You're not a failure.

LOLA: Oh, whatever. Blah, blah, blah. Being here in this horrible, smelly, disgusting apartment. He permeates the walls. Even dead. I wish I had punched him in the face last time I saw him.

BRUNO: He was an old, sick man.

LOLA: Like that's an excuse? He's old, he's sick. He's still a monster. I hope his death was painful and that he suffered.

BRUNO: Shit. You are like all bad Karma.

LOLA: Whatever. If I didn't have my rage, I'd be dead.

(A realization)

Oh, wait.

She starts to laugh. Then cries.

BRUNO: You've gotta let shit go, it's gonna eat you alive.

SANDY *(suddenly, to Bruno)*: Why are you defending him?

BRUNO: I'm not!

SANDY: You are. "Old sick man." Men sticking together. I hope you don't have the same kind of urges. I mean pansexuality, amirite?

LOLA: Uncalled for, Sand!

BRUNO: That's shitty. That's— wow.

He grabs his coat.

SANDY: Running away? Too close to the truth? Enjoy your kinks. At least you get the choice. We were dragged into it. Our sexuality was fucked up from the time we were little girls.

BRUNO exits.

Coward!

SANDY stands, triumphant and then guilty.

I'm going to bed.

SANDY exits. LOLA looks out the window at Bogotá.

LOLA: I hate this goddamned country.

She starts to glow.

A BRILLIANT FLASH OF LIGHT.

AMENDS

LOLA's head is pounding.

LOLA *(to the room)*: Nena. Come out Nena.

A long pause. LOLA toys with the Creepy Jesus. Her head blazes.

I want to die where I was born. To complete the circle. I need to make amends with this country. Please. I know you wanted me here. I see you in dreams. I'm so close to passing over, I don't know what's true here and what lies beyond. Help me. Please.

NENA enters.

LOLA: Nena–

NENA: So you're finally ready to talk?.

LOLA: My head. It's pounding. Oh, god.

NENA: I'm here, mi amor.

LOLA: Make it stop hurting.

NENA: If it stops, you stop.

LOLA: Then take me with you.

NENA: Not yet, mi amor.

NENA sits LOLA down and puts her head in her lap. Lola is not someone used to physical affection. She resists. Nena pats her head. It feels good.

LOLA: I am being punished.

NENA: You don't pray enough.

LOLA: I'm an atheist.

NENA: Yet here you are, repeating the sins of Eve.

LOLA: It's not a sin. To want knowledge.

NENA: Then why do women always pay for it? Does that feel better?

LOLA: I'm seeing sparkles behind my eyes.

NENA: How pretty. Pretend they are stars. That's what I would do after a beating.

LOLA: Nena. I never belonged over there.

NENA: You don't belong here either.

LOLA: My body– I don't think it's going to last very long– I have the cancer. The one that got you.

NENA: Ah. Sí. It starts with constantly being afraid. The body can't fight that.

LOLA: Breasts, bones, brain. I haven't told anyone.

NENA: Good.

LOLA: I couldn't stand it if they were nice to me. Owww. Did you curse me?

NENA: Cómo puedes decir eso? I'll get some ice for your head.

NENA gets up and trips over the cookie tin. It looks like it's about to spill. LOLA dives for it. The two women end up tangled on the floor the tin between them.

What's this?

LOLA: Saúl's ashes. Teresa gave them to me.

NENA laughs. A sounds of wind and a feeling of chains being snapped.

NENA: AH!!! Good girl! And he's really, REALLY dead this time?

LOLA: Yep. He died as he lived. Fucking young girls over.

NENA: Oh Mija. His thing never worked all that well and in the final years he was fully

(Sticks tongue out)

PHBBBT. Teresa's baby isn't his.

LOLA: Lalalalalala. Let's not. Makes my head hurt more. Sing me to sleep, please Nena?

NENA: I will if you do one thing for me. Take a handful of his ashes and put them in the bowl in front of Jesús.

LOLA: Ew. OK.

She opens the cookie tin. Gingerly takes a couple of pinches of ash and places it in the bowl. Jesus glows.

NENA *(singing: La Luna y el Toro)*: Y ese toro enamorado de la luna

Que abandona por la noche la manada

Y el pintado de amapola y aceituna

Y le puso campanero al malloral

LOLA falls asleep. SAÚL enters.

Por fin Saúl! Colorin colora'o este cuento se acaba'o.

SAÚL tries to hit her. He can't. She starts to giggle.

You got some unfinished business, Saúl! But it's not with me! HA!

NENA laughs and laughs.

BLACKOUT.

ILL

NENA's laugh continues. The sound of a weak baby cry. LOLA jerks awake. Starts to retch.

LOLA *(suddenly)*: Oh.

SANDY enters in her pajamas.

SANDY: Are you going to throw up?

LOLA: There's nothing left to throw up.

SANDY: It's the damn lasagna. I think there's some Pedialyte in the bathroom—

LOLA: No, it's fine. Don't worry about me.

SANDY *(frowning; checking Lola's head)*: You have a fever.

LOLA: Please. I'm fine. It's probably a flashback or something. Bad dream, the baby-

She sits with her sadness.

SANDY: Try and sleep. Do you want an Ativan?

LOLA: No. I'm trying to stay clean.

NENA has appeared at the door. She is cutting out her paper dolls.

NENA: Porque?

SANDY: Ok. Just relax, ok, I know, this place—

LOLA: Yeah. Yeah. I'm fine.

SANDY exits.

NENA: Tragedy always happens to the eldest. A long, long line.

LOLA: My therapist says my tragedies are of my own making. Even my baby.

NENA: I'm sorry I wasn't around to help you.

LOLA: Poor little guy. I never really wanted a kid. But, I don't know, it seemed like I needed to make up for the one I got rid of when I was sixteen.

NENA: Do you want to see him?

LOLA: No. Oh my god. No. No. I want him to be in another body, a good one this time with a nice strong heart. I want his soul to be running around with other kids. In Canada, where kids don't get shot every day. I'm lucky I lost him when he was so tiny. What if he HAD lived? And then he got shot in his first-grade classroom. Or he survived that and then died in a car crash on his 16th birthday?

NENA: Oye, Mi'ja. Maybe you should take this Ativan that Sandy recommended. You are muy deprimida.

LOLA: The darkness is real.

NENA: Ya. Enough. Carajo. We all thought moving you children to Norte America would take you towards the light.

LOLA: Except that there we are always "The Other."

NENA: You could've passed for white! You always have to trumpet your damn, cómo se dice, Latinidad. Que estupidez!

LOLA: I'm proud of my heritage!

NENA: It doesn't make you special. Why aren't you quiet about it?

LOLA: I'm not the one who makes a thing of it! It's my entire industry. I finally get a chance to put together my own TV show and it gets reviewed by Whitey McFuckface, who opens with the charming, and not at all offensive, "Sombreros off to this Hispanic showrunner"— I've been put in the box by other people. Including you.

NENA: No! Cómo puedes decir eso?

LOLA: You told me how happy you were that I was "blanquita" unlike my "Indio" brother. Joke's on you. I did that DNA thing. I'm 33 percent indigenous. Thirty-three percent!

NENA: No, de donde? Es de lado de tu papá.

LOLA: That's exactly what Mami said!

NENA: Blood of the invader, blood of the invaded. Born of rape and murder and pain. If we let that mierda define us, we'll never pull out of it.

LOLA: Mierda does define me.

NENA: Ay, mi madre. Intolerable! You are a pura Norte Americana! Always examining your belly button and thinking the lint explains your soul.

LOLA: I don't LIKE feeling this way.

NENA: Puro carajo. You DO. You LOVE feeeeeeling. You are all the sins of the world wrapped up in one insecure yet arrogant ball of humanity.

LOLA: I'm not insecure!

NENA: Oh yes, and stubborn. Mean. Self-aggrandizing and tragic. Yes. That "chekís" a lot of boxes.

LOLA: You are a fucking evil brain tumor.

NENA: Ha! Hahahahah!

She chortles merrily. The apartment seems to breathe. NENA takes the cover off the creepy Jesus. JESUS smiles.

LOLA: Is he going to talk to me?

NENA: I don't know, child, he's your psychosis not mine.

JESUS: Hola, mija.

LOLA is only slightly surprised that Jesus speaks.

LOLA: Hola.

JESUS: Where have you been?

LOLA: I've been here.

JESUS: This morning was your first day back in church in about 20 years, no?

LOLA: No. Mom's funeral.

JESUS: That was non-denominational. Doesn't count. Come back into the arms of the church, sweet child.

NENA *(scolding)*: Jesús. Déjala. She's going through a lot and she doesn't need you and your crazy guilt trips.

JESUS *(pleasantly)*: Ok. So hell and damnation it is. Have a blast Dolores!

LOLA: Thanks, I hear it's more fun there.

JESUS: Whatever. You think the devil has Lou Reed and Prince? Nah. They're all ours. You can hang out with Justin Bieber. [Or any equally annoying current pop star]

LOLA: He's dead?

JESUS: Not yet.

LOLA *(trying to shake it off)*: No. No. No. I refuse to do magical realism. It's bullshit, high concept and no.

JESUS *(under the doll)*: But you're the Latina in the room! Isn't that what you do??

LOLA: What I do is write better than 90 percent of the mediocre white men in the industry for half the money.

JESUS: Damn. Man hater.

LOLA: Men are trash.

JESUS: Women don't have a sense of humor.

LOLA: Oh we do. It's just evolved past 7th grade. Watch?

LOLA does a pratfall. JESUS laughs.

See? Slapstick. Me fall down go boom. I like my humor more— sophisticated.

JESUS: Yeah, right. You used to watch El Chavo Del Ocho every day!

LOLA: I was eight! Ok, fine. Men literally torture each other, ha-ha, isn't his morbid obesity highlarious!? Oh damn. Now he's dead. Our bad. OH MY GOD. Men aren't funny, they're cruel.

JESUS: Oh, Mijita. Hell is full of comedians, you definitely don't want to end up there.

(A beat change)

I'm good at jokes, you want to hear a joke?

He has shaken the doll off his head.

LOLA:
No!

NENA:
Si!

JESUS: Jesus walks into a restaurant, asks for a table for 26, the waitress says, "There's only 13 of you?" Jesus says, yeah, but we're all going to sit on the same side.

JESUS waits expectantly for applause.

Jesus points to the bread, "This is my body." He points to the wine. "This is my blood." He points to the mayo— Judas says "I'm going to stop you right there."

NENA and LOLA groan.

What's the difference between me and a picture of me? It only takes one nail to hang up the picture! Hahahah!!!

An appalled pause.

If you can't laugh at yourself—?

LOLA *(to Nena)*: Well, now we know humor is a human invention.

JESUS: I am omnipotent!

NENA: Doesn't mean you're funny.

JESUS pouts.

JESUS: I died for your sins.

LOLA: I don't sin. I'm just a collection of atoms and neurons.

JESUS: Blasphemer!

LOLA: You're a myth!

JESUS *(enjoying this)*: Straight to hell!!!

(Singing to the tune of "Ring my Bell:)

Straight— to— he- he- hellllll, straight to hell.

LOLA: You know, I like you. It's your dad I can't stand.

JESUS: Ever since that priest made you kiss his— ring, you've been impossible.

NENA puts the cozy on JESUS. They struggle. It becomes a shoving match, but Nena gets the cozy on his head.

LOLA *(like a lightning strike, her head pounds)*: Ow. Ow. OOOWW.

(A pause)

Damn it. I'm hungry. Again.

NENA: Let's have a party!

LOLA: It's like I've never eaten before. I'm going to get huge.

JESUS *(from under the cozy)*: Let me out! I want to be friends.

LOLA: No you don't. You're like a lousy L.A. boyfriend, you want me to worship you, so you can make me feel bad. I feel bad enough.

NENA: He won't hurt you.

LOLA removes the cozy.

LOLA: OK.

(To Jesus)

But no more jokes.

JESUS: Get me out of this place. I want to see the stars!

BRUNO enters. He sees LOLA playing with Jesus.

BRUNO: Girl. What'chu you doing with that??

LOLA: Finding Jesus?

BRUNO: Freak.

BRUNO waves his hand dismissively. Sits on the couch in the middle of the action and opens his laptop. NENA watches him.

NENA: This boy is a giant! Born in America, same blood, and he comes out six foot three and hairy like a monster.

BRUNO starts to type furiously, fast. He turns the volume up on his earbuds.

Don't tell him, but he reminds me in his way of my diablo husband. Quiet. Don't know what goes on behind his eyes.

LOLA: He didn't talk till he was five. Some gringo doctor told my mom he was retarded.

JESUS: Good thing you were in El Norte. Here, he'd be a broken toy.

LOLA: He's on the spectrum. But high, you know. He's smarter than all of us, but way too sensitive.

BRUNO *(hears this; suspicious)*: Who are you talking to?

LOLA *(grabbing her phone)*: I'm, uh, dictating for a new pilot.

BRUNO: Can you please disguise me better? It's fucking embarrassing. I get all these DMs from your fans asking me if I really have a 12 inch—

They laugh together.

LOLA: You should pay me a finders fee.

BRUNO: True dat.

He makes a muscle.

Make me buffer this time.

LOLA rolls her eyes.

NENA: I like him. He's funny.

LOLA: And smart. He doesn't seem to be looking for love all the time.

NENA: Only women really want love.

LOLA: UGH. Whiny, needy and boring. Men must want love too.

BRUNO: Men want to have sex, get fed and be left alone.

LOLA: Duh. Basic. I always got it so wrong. That's why no one loved me

BRUNO goes back to work.

JESUS: Andrew loved you.

LOLA: Yeah, OK.

NENA: He's a good man. Good choice too, the big, white conquistador.

LOLA: Oh shit. I fell for the patriarchy!

BRUNO: Hey Lo, do you want to go clubbing tonight?

LOLA: Clubbing. Like seals, or dancing?

BRUNO: Don't be stupid. Look:

He shows her his computer.

"Vintrash." It's in an old guerrilla stronghold, they converted it into a dance club.

LOLA: That's pretty sick.

BRUNO: I know. Wait, sick good? Or sick gross?

LOLA: Both.

BRUNO: It's "Gringo Tuesday," we'll fit right in!

BRUNO sticks his earbuds back in.

NENA: He's surrounded by angels.

LOLA *(affectionately)*: I know. He's always been so, so lucky. That's a big reason Sandy can't stand him. He's always doing dangerous shit and getting away with it.

BRUNO *(interjecting)*: My shit is not dangerous. It's adventurous.

SANDY enters. She is dragging an old suitcase.

SANDY: Look what I found it under the maid's bed! It's locked.

NENA: It's mine, I hid it there.

BRUNO: Here.

He hands Lola a multi-tool.

LOLA *(giving Sandy the tool)*: Here?

SANDY *(contemptuous)*: Ugh.

She opens it as if it's covered in plague. BRUNO flips a middle finger. SANDY works but can't open the suitcase. NENA comes over and opens it. It bursts, spilling out pictures and memorabilia,

Who are these people?

NENA: Your family. Our family.

SANDY: Here's the asshole.

Passes a picture over to LOLA.

LOLA: He wasn't terrible looking.

SANDY looks at her like she's lost her mind.

SANDY: Medals, passports, huh, Anna Karenina? Ooh—

SANDY picks up a picture of group of children.

NENA: Mis hermanos!

LOLA: My god. These are all brothers and sisters? I don't even want to imagine what great-grandma's vajayjay looked like at the end.

SANDY: Like the Grand Canyon. One, two— eight. Nine. Nine.

NENA: Out of 11. Nine that lived.

LOLA: Christ on a cracker.

JESUS: Respeto!!

SANDY and BRUNO almost hear JESUS.

LOLA: I'm lucky if I can muster the interest once a month.

NENA: She didn't have much of a choice.

SANDY picks up another picture.

SANDY: Oh. Nena and Saúl's wedding picture.

NENA: I had just turned 15. He was almost 40. And completely useless. Look way in the bottom.

LOLA pulls out a wrapped package. It's an old revolver. It glows.

BRUNO: Don't get your fingerprints on it!

SANDY: This isn't CSI.

BRUNO: It could be a murder weapon.

NENA: Americans and their gun obsession.

LOLA: Stop calling us Americans.

LOLA unwraps the gun and holds it.

BRUNO *(mad)*: Quit it! I'm the Columbine generation, dude, you're giving me PTSD.

BRIGHT FLASH OF LIGHT.

SAÚL enters. The following should be fast and slapsticky:

SAÚL *(very charming)*: You brought all the nietos? Que lindos.

(To Nena)

Ya vete. No one needs you here anymore.

NENA *(hiding behind Jesus; taunting Saúl)*: Leave them alone!

SAÚL: Cállate!

NENA *(sticks her tongue out)*: No! PPPPPHHHHTTTTT.

SAÚL: They came to say goodbye to me!!

NENA: Estás loco? Te odian!!

SAÚL *(goes to hit her!)*: Te voy a–

JESUS *(very loudly and powerful)*: Quit it!!

The last sentence is said loudly enough to make SANDY and BRUNO jump. LOLA turns and sees SAÚL.

BRUNO:
Did that head just–?

JESUS:
One more word out of you and I'm stopping this universe and taking you home!

NENA:
Lolita!

SAÚL:
Mi Lola.

LOLA points the gun at SAÚL. She tries to hide behind SANDY, who is trying to get the gun. BRUNO is trying to avoid the gun. It's chaos.

SAÚL: Qué haces con mi pistola, mi linda?

SANDY *(to Lola, re: the gun)*: Whoa! Give me that!

NENA: Saúl, déjala en paz!

SAÚL *(to Nena)*: Que fea eres. Seca como el desierto y tu corazón.

JESUS: That's a month in purgatory, Saúl!

Everyone is moving way too fast.

LOLA *(shaking, to Saúl)*: I'm not scared of you.

SAÚL: Why should you be scared of me? You were my favorite.

LOLA: Fuck you!!

SANDY: Whoa! Crazy pants. Give me the gun!\

BRUNO *(scared out of his mind)*: Stop messin'. It won't shoot, right? It's too old. Right? Right!!?\

SANDY: Lo– C'mon. Give it to me.\

SAÚL: Preciosa.\

LOLA tries to shoot the gun. It falls apart in her hands.

JESUS: Now how is it going to kill someone in the last scene? Why can't you follow the rules, Lola?

LOLA *(a realization)*: I make the rules!

(To Saúl)

And you can't touch me!

SAÚL *(hurt)*: Bueno, if not you, then the little one. She was always quieter anyway.

He turns to SANDY. LOLA dives to protect Sandy, and lands in the suitcase. She flings a handful of paper dolls at SAÚL. Paper dolls start to fly out of the suitcase, more than could possibly be inside. They come out newsprint, and then red, red, red. They tangle Lola up in them.

LOLA: Leave her alone!

Her head blazes.

OOOWWW!!!

The earth shakes.

JESUS: Ay Díos YO. Now you've done it.

NENA: Secrets. Too many secrets. You let them out—

JESUS: You'll never get them back in, Pandora!

LOLA *(her head blazes)*: So much pain, woman after girl after child. So many, too many—\

SAÚL:
Secretos!

NENA:
Secrets!

SANDY: Lola, breathe!\

The earth shakes again, but much harder. LOLA and SANDY scream. BRUNO freaks out.

BRUNO: QUAKE!!!!\

SAÚL: Por qué no me quieren?!\

JESUS does a full on juju on the room. SAÚL, SANDY, and BRUNO freeze.

JESUS: Díos ex machina, activate! Lets go!

The door opens.

LOLA: What. No!\

NENA: Lola, follow Jesús. Hurry\

LOLA picks up the Creepy Jesus.

JESUS *(to Lola)*: You look terrible. When was your last confession?

LOLA: When I was eight. I told you he touched me and you told me I needed to pray about it.\

NENA *(to Saúl)*: Goodbye. I may never get to heaven but at least I can get out of here.

LOLA: I can't leave Sandy here with Saúl!

NENA: You have to. She's the only one who can do something about him. Vamos!

LOLA *(to Sandy)*: I'm sorry, Sandy. I've always let you down. Good luck.

LOLA hands SANDY the pieces of the gun and exits.

JESUS *(like a referee)*: And go!

JESUS exits with NENA, who whoops with joy at crossing the threshold. SAÚL can't follow. He turns to BRUNO. On the unfreeze SANDY suddenly sees Saúl.

SAÚL: Chiquis. Y mira! El niño!

SANDY: Oh my god!

SAÚL: Que bueno que tuvieron baron. A man to carry on the tradition.

SAÚL goes to embrace BRUNO. Bruno spellbound starts to fall into Saúl's arms.

SANDY: Get away from him!!

SANDY runs to stop the embrace. She puts her body physically between SAÚL and BRUNO.

BRUNO: What the hell!?

SANDY shoves BRUNO out the door.

SANDY: Bruno, go, get out of here, quickly!

BRUNO *(the spell broken; He starts to have an asthma attack)*: —I can't breathe. oh shit oh shit oh—

SANDY: Run!!

SANDY shoves BRUNO out the door, tries to go after him. The door slams. Her fear is palpable. SAÚL laughs.

It took 40,000 hours of work to become a doctor. I am analytical. I am a scientist. I rejected the demons long ago. I will not run. I will not hide.

She sobs once.

I refuse to succumb to fantasy or despair. Logic is the only way I survive.

Saúl comes towards her.

Stay away. Stay the hell away!

SAÚL *(laughing, charming, scary)*: Niña. Muñequita. You're so pretty. Smile, muñeca—

SANDY *(furious)*: Don't tell me to smile!!

He goes to touch her, she slaps his hand away. Suddenly, his whole body reels with a hard and painful electric shock.

SAÚL: Ay!

It really hurts.

(Surprised)

Ay, hijo de puta.

SANDY: Oh. Oh!

Scared but determined, she touches him. The electric shock. He grimaces.

SAÚL: Pare! Me duele!

SANDY: Ha!

She pokes him, hard. A doubly violent and vicious electric shock courses through SAÚL.

SAÚL: Ay!!!

SANDY, astonished, starts to laugh hysterically.

BLACKOUT.

JESUS IN HIS TEMPLE

LOLA and NENA sitting on the edge of what seems like a great height. The JESUS HEAD is next to them. Stars sparkle overhead. They watch the sky. A shooting star appears.

NENA: Oh! Una estrella fugaz! I wish—

She wishes. LOLA frets.

LOLA: God. I'm so weak. I feel guilty, leaving Sandy there with him.

NENA: He isn't yours to deal with.

Another star.

Vaya, niña.

LOLA: I don't know what to wish for.

NENA: Wish for good health.

LOLA: Not gonna happen. I wish I was less of a fuck up—

NENA: You can't wish for a negative.

LOLA: I wish that my husband—

JESUS: You're not married.

NENA: They love each other! It's enough.

LOLA: I never wanted to get married, but now that we're broken up, I miss being his fake wife.

JESUS: Did you pay any attention in Catechism? It's a sacrament, not some hipster institution.

NENA: Mijita. You're allowed to have love. Andrew was good to you.

LOLA: My wish is that Drew finds someone else, a little 27 year-old boopsie girl that will worship him and give him the kid he deserves.

JESUS: Hell, hell, hell. Young women and old men.

LOLA: Dude. Your mom was 13.

JESUS: Women are fertile at that age.

LOLA: We're not women yet. We're little blobs of hormones and neediness.

NENA: I was 15 when I got married.

LOLA: Marriage is institutionalized madness.

Another shooting star.

NENA: There's another one.

LOLA *(to Jesus)*: Your turn to make a wish.

The JESUS HEAD thinks.

JESUS: I'd like world peace.

LOLA: Isn't that like one of your superpowers?

JESUS: No, Mi'ja! You think the Jews or the Hindus or the Americans are going to listen to me?

LOLA: Touché, creepy.

LOLA looks out over Bogotá.

Bogotá is so beautiful. All the lights, the fires. The way the industrial center leads to the utter poverty on the edges. The way it blurs centuries. That's Latin America. Poverty and luxury side by side, and unapologetic.

NENA: Don't romanticize. We are poor people here. Poor beyond imagination. And Bogotá is cold. A cold place in the real and in the after. I miss the sea and Puerto Colombia.

LOLA: Oh! Bis-Abuela's old place! It was magic. The dirt floors, the cracked walls. The endless kittens. The fish in the well. A well! And the tortoises.

NENA: The tortoises.

JESUS: Tortoises have beautiful souls.

LOLA: Mami went back right before she got too sick to travel. I should've gone with her. She texted a ton of pictures. It was so, so small. Except for the tortoises, they were just as big as I remembered.

JESUS: Your Bis-Abuela disappointed me. Going Jehovah's Witness after so many good years!

They all pause. Thinking.

LOLA *(hesitating)*: Nena?

NENA: Mmmm?

LOLA: You stopped praying when the doctor diagnosed you with cancer. After a lifetime of praying every day, almost all day.

NENA: Praying. I guess I asked for too much. I used up all of my credit con Díos.

JESUS: You did ask for a lot.

NENA: A lifetime spent begging. How many bargains did I make with God? I knew he would exact a price. But it got your Mami to America, and away from Saúl and this hard, cold place with it's hard, cold gods. When cancer came to get me I stopped praying because I knew God was taking his cut. And now—

She sighs.

Still disentangling mistakes made years and years ago.

LOLA: I'm so angry at you.

NENA: Your fury makes you whole.

LOLA: I am not whole. I'm a broken doll. And it's your fault.

NENA: Lolita—

LOLA: Why didn't you protect us from him? Why, Nena? You knew how he was, and you LET him be alone with us.

NENA: Ay! Why is it always about ese viejo—? He was a bully, just a bully, nothing more interesting than that. I only studied until I was 12, but I wasn't dumb like him. My father used to read Russian novels to me! But my failed military man was no romantic figure. Look at our wedding picture. He's so weak he's leaning against the wall. My mother thought our union would do us both good.

JESUS: Because you were so wild. She had to tie you down, tame you.

NENA: He got so frustrated that he couldn't perform on our wedding night. There was blood on the sheets, but it was from my bloodied nose. Everyone joked about how spirited I must've been. I guess I was too old for him at 15.

LOLA: What makes a man sexually aroused by little girls. It's so fucking wrong. I thought that's why we got boobs, and huge asses. Why little girls?

NENA: I don't know. But it happens to all of us. Every little girl I knew. Every woman. I don't know why you Americans have to make such a fuss about it.

LOLA: Because it's wrong.

NENA: That's you being modern. I didn't like it, no one does, but what choice did we have? If it wasn't the old man. It would have been someone else.

LOLA: It's been a lot of someone elses.

NENA: But you broke the pattern. You got angry. You fought back. If I had had a choice I would have swum in the ocean all day. I was the fastest swimmer. No one could catch me, though plenty tried. I could've competed in los Olympics

She laughs. So does JESUS.

JESUS: Not in the nude, the way you used to do it.

NENA: My body was poetry. Too bad I was born a woman and not a dolphin.

JESUS: Don't be blasphemous. I answered a lot of your prayers. I got you out of his house

NENA: It took 30 years!

(To Lola)

When your mother brought me to the US, my life opened up like an orchid on the branch. America! Snow!

LOLA: You loved snow.

NENA: It made me laugh.

LOLA: You're dead! You could be anywhere! Why don't you go where it snows?

NENA: Saúl made me swear on everything I found holy that I would bury him, but— oops—! I left my body on earth 20 years before he did. That bastard just wouldn't give! He had three different cancers, lost a kidney! Heart attacks galore! He died twice right in front of me!

NENA (CONT'D): The first time he died at the hospital, I thought, "Finally, I am free of his curse!" I was already picking up my purse and signing the funeral papers when he inhaled hard and sat bolt upright. All his skin fell off, and he had a terrified look on his face. "Vi el diablo! Vi el diablo!" He was so scared of the devil, he refused to die. The second time he died, the doctors assured me he was flat-lined and they even got as far as the morgue, but — POOMinhale! And back he came. Scared the coroner half to death. I knew then, I was in deep trouble.

LOLA: That's why you're here?

NENA *(deflecting)*: Eh. I don't know where to go yet.

JESUS: It won't be heaven, you know.

NENA: I'd like to come back as a tortoise.

LOLA: You're waiting for me to join you.

NENA: Eso crées?

LOLA: I'm really sick Nena.

NENA: Mijita, when you die people will remember your name! Those little, cómo se dice, nerds, will cry and make los memes and send los tweets. But, I don't think you've done everything you have left to do.

(Prodding)

Right, Jesus?

JESUS: I have nothing to do with it. The cords of fate are cut on your birth. And yes, I'm aware that's a Greek myth. Religion isn't supposed to make sense.

The trio sit watching the stars. A whole bunch of shooting stars appear. They close their eyes and wish.

LIGHT SHIFT.

THE VIAL

SANDY has a bottle of wine and is swigging from it. SAÚL stands uncomfortably. Sandy is laughing. She occasionally pokes Saúl for fun. It's cruel, unhinged, and very satisfying.

SAÚL *(begging)*: Please, pare, ya.

SANDY: You're kind of a loser ghost. You're supposed to be scary.

SAÚL: You were scared of me?

SANDY: I know!!

(Poke)

Lo and I made you out to be such a monster.

SAÚL: I'm not a monster! Why did you come, if you think so poorly of me?

SANDY: My therapist said it would be good closure.

(Poke. Poke. Poke.)

SAÚL: AAAYY!! No hay such thing as closure.

SANDY: Mira, viejo, that time Mom asked me to come help you deal with your doctors?

She reaches into her pocket. Takes out a little bag. Holds up a vial of blood.

I took more than was needed.

Shows him the vial.

This is your double-helix, your DNA.

SAÚL: Mi que?

SANDY: A part of you is still alive, see, and I took it into my group therapy session and the other women and I decided that I should do a symbolic exorcism when I got here. I guess it's not so symbolic tho./

She pokes him, he yells.

Damn. That is unbelievably satisfying. You understand?

SAÚL: I understand. I understand that cruelty doesn't skip generations.

She takes another thing out of the bag.

SANDY: Look, Saúl. From your pillow, hair. From the bed, flakes of skin and sore. From the toothbrush, from the dentures. You, you, you. Thanks to modern science and a little witchcraft you're my bitch now, baby!

SANDY shakes the vial. SAÚL feels every shake.

SAÚL: No.

SANDY *(menacing, unhinged)*: Bwahahahaha!!! I've captured your soul. Where will I take you?

SAÚL: I have to stay here in this apartment or I will go to the devil. I'm not leaving.

SANDY: The torments of hell are all you deserve. You were a shitty person.

SAÚL: Let Teresa have me. She promised to pray over my soul.

SANDY: Why? So you can torture her, and poison her children? No, Saúl. I'd like to destroy you but your energy has to go somewhere. Theory of entropy and all that.

SAÚL: I've been stuck here for thousands of years. Millenia. I am ancient.

SANDY: A demon? A malignant spirit. No, you're just an old man.

SAÚL *(sincerely, pleading)*: I was beaten as a child. My mother used to grab me by the head and fling me against walls. She once tied a belt around my neck and tried to hang me and herself.

SANDY *(stopped by this; Pretends to be unmoved)*: We are all products of trauma.

SAÚL: Oye, niña. That American, come se dice, pop-schyc-o-logy, it's all mierda y excuses.

SANDY: It's science, burro. In our DNA. Our pain, our rapes, our anguish lives on in our blood, and passes it down to our children. You could've stopped.

SAÚL: I— it was my right. Nena is my wife. I bought her. And the child was mine to do with as I wished.

SANDY: Your own little girl—

SAÚL: Little girls are so flirtatious. What's a man to think?

SANDY, enraged, grabs SAÚL by the ears. The violent shock sends him flying to the floor.

SANDY: This is why I won't bring a little girl into this world. Unless I destroy you and everyone like you.

SAÚL: You're a lunatic!

SANDY: Naw. I'm a fixer. And you need to be fixed.

SAÚL: Why isn't the story of my childhood filling you with compassion?

SANDY: Welp. We all had shitty childhoods, buddy. Some of us don't become kid rapists. Compassion!

She snort/hiccups.

I have no pity for your, poor me, I had a toxic upbringing and I needed to prove my manly man worth. I'm not crying one tear.

SAÚL *(clearly uncomfortable)*: Oye. Pero, that's as sick as me, no?

SANDY: Y que? I'm not allowed to be pissed and evil? That's only for dudes?

SAÚL: Women are supposed to protect the world from us!

SANDY: Oh, so I'm the angel of vengeance? I like that!

SAÚL: Please, you're crazy. Just give me to Tere. I don't belong to you.

SANDY: Tere gave us your ashes. She's done with your ass too.

SAÚL: Puta!

SANDY plays with the vial of blood. Drinks her wine. Sits and watches SAÚL. Bemused.

SANDY: I sure enjoy watching you squirm.

SAÚL: Aren't you angry at your sister for leaving me to you?

SANDY: Shaddup.

She takes another big drink. Lifts her glass to cheer. Pokes him again.

Lo AA'd you outta her system. Or whatever the fuck she did to get sober.

She stares at her wine.

I guess I'm finally ready to deal with you. But it's going to be on my terms, viejo.

She looks at him. Makes a decision. Takes another huge slug.

Fuck it! I feel like dancing!

SAÚL: Que? NO!

SANDY turns on some loud music, she dances with abandon, poking SAÚL for fun.

SANDY: Does it hurt, does it hurt, does it hurt?

SAÚL yelps each time she pokes. But he's trapped. He's frustrated with his inability to hurt SANDY. He yowls.

SAÚL: This isn't fair! This isn't fair! I'm your family!

SANDY: Dance, viejo, dance on your grave! You want mercy? Dance!

SANDY dances unhinged. SAÚL, reluctant, does the same.

LIGHT SHIFT.

IGLESIA

The light changes to the beautiful and intense brightness of midday Bogotá in front of the old church. BRUNO stands dressed in black. TERE is standing next to him.

BRUNO: Thank you for everything. Um. I'm sorry the priest won't let you into the church.

TERE shrugs.

I had a great time last night. That club was insane.

(A pause)

What are you going to do now? K vas hacer?

TERESA: Quién sabe? Mejor bailar que llorar.

BRUNO: Bailar que— what?

TERE dances.

Llorar—?

She pretends to cry.

Huh. Dancing makes you cry? Sorry. I know I'm a sucky dancer. My hips don't do the whole swish-swish thing.

Tere rolls her eyes.

Anyway. It was cool of you to hang out with me. And to bring me back home. I guess I got a little blotto. My sisters make me crazy. They talk too much. Thanks for actually listening. Although I don't know if it counts if you can't understand me.

TERESA *(very, VERY fast)*: Mira gringo, ese viejo es un éspiritu maligno. Yo nunca pude saber sí Saúl era mi papá o no, pero sospecho que si era.

BRUNO: Ye—ah. Can you go a little slower— Saúl—papá??!!

TERESA *(very fast)*: Mi mamá siempre me dijo que uno tenia que darle respeto a sus parientes y a la iglesia. Los miro a ustedes, q ni al abuelo, ni a la patria, y ni a Díos son fieles, pero tienen plata, tienen privilegio, tienen el lujo de tener morales. No entiendo nada.

(In a huff)

Ojalá que Díos los arrojen al río! Chao. Espero que no verlos nunca más.

She exits as SANDY enters. TERE scowls and passes her without a word. Sandy is in the same clothes she wore the night before, reeking of sweat and alcohol, which Bruno notices. Her head pounds. She carries the cookie tin under her arm. A long uncomfortable silence. Then:

BRUNO: So, we ARE having a funeral. Father A took the money. We got a 20-minute slot. The relatives WhatsApp-ed each other and there are like 50 people I barely know in there. Waiting for us. To bury the dude. Who's in a cookie tin. Shit.

SANDY: Oh. Where'd Teresa go?

BRUNO: The priest wouldn't let her stay.

SANDY: That's sexist bullshit.

BRUNO: Uh— Teresa and I had a... uh... I guess a date. I guess? But— shit. A.) Sloppy seconds from my dead grandpa, and B) POSSIBLY a relative.

SANDY: A relative?

BRUNO: His. Kid. I think.

SANDY: Shit.

BRUNO: Yeah. Too bad, she's really cute.

SANDY: AAAAUUGHHH! You're just as bad as he was!

BRUNO: My god. Take a joke.

SANDY: It's not fucking funny.

A long pause. SANDY, experimenting, pokes BRUNO. He reacts, annoyed:

BRUNO: Hey! What the—

SANDY: Just checking.

BRUNO: Keep your hands to yourself. I didn't give you permission to touch me.

SANDY: Permission?

She snorts.

BRUNO: Yeah. It's called consent. I know you think I'm dense or whatever, but I saw how fucked up Lola was because of what happened, I worked hard not to be like him.

SANDY *(offering the cookie tin)*: Do you want a cookie for not being a rapist?

BRUNO *(maybe upset, maybe clear eyed)*: Goddamit! —I'm fighting the pull. I feel it, pushing behind my eyes, filling my body. Telling me I'm the conqueror, I need to take what I want, and if it's scared of me? Even better. I'm supposed to be a fucking jaguar, ripping the throat out of my prey. The minute I got my first hard-on, I knew how fucked up it all was. But I'm not gonna lie. I like sex. Sex is good. Sex is fun. Sex is a fucking great hobby. But I'm not toxic, I never hurt anyone. Never forced myself on anyone. I'm nothing like him. I could be, I know that, but I'm not.

SANDY: I think that's more words than you've spoken to me in the last ten years.

BRUNO: Dude. There's a whole world of consensual sex out there, Sandy, a world I am happy to inhabit. I could give you some websites to check out—

SANDY: No. Thank. You.

BRUNO: —BTDubs I get tested on the reg and I've never had an STD, no thanks to your rude pamphlet drop. And I do it all the time with all kinds of folx, Yeah, men, women, non-binary, genderqueer, kinks, furries—

SANDY: Yeah. You had the freedom of skipping the bullshit. We didn't.

BRUNO *(still frustrated)*: Are you ever going to listen?

SANDY: Not my job to make you feel better about MY abuse.

She holds her ground. BRUNO tries to say something else. Gives up. A pause.

BRUNO *(checks her watch)*: Damn it. We have to go. There's a baptism in 30. Where is she?

SANDY: Lola's such a drama queen.

BRUNO: She hated him.

SANDY: Everyone hated him. But what a will to live! He had cancer everywhere. EVERYWHERE. And he outlived Nena by 20 years and Mom by 2.

BRUNO: And now we are stuck pretending we gave a shit about the old fart. Do we get anything?

SANDY: What do you mean, "get"?

BRUNO: Money?

SANDY: Are you kidding? I guess one of us gets Creepy Jesus.

BRUNO: And the apartment.

SANDY: Ugh.

(Shudders)

Let's give it to Teresa.

BRUNO: Co-sign.

SANDY & BRUNO: I'll talk Lola into it.

A very, very small moment of understanding.

SANDY *(seeing someone waving)*: Shit. There's the priest! Let's get this over with.

BRUNO: What about Lo?

SANDY: She's fine. Unless she's dead. And if she's dead, we'll deal with it later. And if she's not dead, maybe I'll kill her.

They exit. LOLA comes out of hiding wearing the most colorful clothing imaginable. Completely inappropriate for a funeral. Lola holds the JESUS head. She sets it down. NENA enters a beat later.

JESUS: Go in there and dance for me.

LOLA: Really?

JESUS: Sure, why not. I have to change to be relevant, no?

LOLA *(pointing at her clothes)*: I'm not dressed right.

NENA: I think you look great. Very dramatica, like something out of a magazine.

LOLA: If that's what you want. They already think I'm nuts.

JESUS: You are nuts.

LOLA *(picking up her skirts)*: I think I'll run in. Singing.

Maybe she sings something that sounds like "Like a Virgin."

JESUS: A little on the nose.

NENA: I love it. Shake it on the altar.

JESUS: Kids today.

NENA: Vaya. Rápido antes de que te arrepientas.

LOLA: I got nothing to repent for. C'mon J-man.

She picks up the head.

JESUS: Seriously? I thought you didn't believe in an afterlife.

LOLA: Well. I don't. But— I guess I'll hedge my bets.

(To Nena)

You're not coming in?

NENA: I won't step foot in that church. We got married in there. Bad memories! I'll be just outside the door, waiting, Lolita.

JESUS *(to Lola)*: Alright, baby. Let's rock and roll. Give these gatos a thriller-diller!

LOLA: Wow. You're such a nerd. Let's go!

LOLA takes off at a full run into the church, the opening beats of a song that might be Madonna's getting louder and louder. As Lola turns around to face the audience, it becomes the pews of an old incense filled church. SANDY and BRUNO are standing on the altar.

SANDY: —Gracias Padre Arévalo, y uh, familia—

LOLA: Stop!

SANDY & BRUNO: Oh, shit.

LOLA *(loudly)*: Hola gente!!! Soy Dolores. Pain! Ha. My name means pain, so you can imagine what my life was like!

She sets the JESUS head down, on the altar where he can watch.

JESUS: Honey. Your name means "sorrow."

LOLA: It does?

JESUS: Spanish 101.

SANDY: Geez, thanks for joining us.

LOLA takes over the service.

LOLA: I come to bury the dead, the past and everybody's expectations.

BRUNO *(working his phone)*: Oooh. Let's get this shit on LIVE.

LOLA *(at the camera)*: Holla!! My name is Lola and I am an— well clearly, alcohol, drugs, sex, etc, etc. Everything to excess or why bother, right? Hah. Uh.

(To Jesus)

They're staring at me.

JESUS: Uh— yes. You're a loony-toon.

LOLA: Cool. Thanks Jesus! Can we get a round of applause for Jesus. This creepy head has been in my family for a long time! Since the conquistadors, probably!

JESUS giggles maniacally, and does a kooky gesture as he gets applause.

This won't take long. I know most of you, though if I'm honest it's mostly from accidentally friending you on Facebook? How many Maria Dolores' does our family need? Anyway. Are we actually mourning this motherfucker? Raise your hands if it's a yes. Oh my god. Put your hands down. Seriously? Ok. Raise your hands if the old fella fondled you when you were little.

She raises a hand. SANDY raises her hand. An uncomfortable murmur.

Hmmm. So just the two Americans? Somehow? No one else? Cool cool cool.

JESUS *(to the congregation)*: You aren't supposed to lie in church. That's a week of purgatory for at least 15 of you.

LOLA: No. Don't punish them. Don't. Secret keeping is our lifeline as women. It's how we survive. I have lots of secrets.

BRUNO: No you don't!

LOLA: Oh I do though! I know it looks like I vomit everything about myself all the time. But, I have secrets. My biggest secret is that I'm dead. I died a few weeks ago.

SANDY: What are you—

The murmur in the church gets louder, at first like an angry crowd but then more like the sound of the sea.

JESUS: You're only slightly dead.

The music starts to pulse. The church lights up like a disco.

LOLA *(dancing)*: I don't know why Saúl felt compelled to use my body or my sister's body. I've been talking about it so long that the idea has lost its bite. Yes, I was molested, but so was, I don't know, EVERY other woman in here? I mean. All of us?

LOLA (CONT'D): And we all turn a blind eye and let him do what he did, and I honestly can't figure out why, or if anyone said to him "stop," or if you all just sighed and figured it was inevitable. I turn that over and over in my head. The mundanity of it. The casual use of my body. Her body. Our bodies. Nothing but holes and mounds and weakness and lies. The biggest lie, and the one that makes my bones ache, is that our lives as women are worth nothing. Our history's erased. Our lives forgotten. I'm here to tell you that we are EVERYTHING. Goddesses of creation, motherfuckers! This body:

She takes off her dress and stands, lovely in her underwear (which might be Wonder Women Underoos).

This body creates life, multitasks like nobody's business, is a hella great writer, and can hold me up here, even as it's full of cancer and death. Full of cancer like him. But unlike him, I'm not afraid to die.

She raises her fist.

Here's to the old man! Celebrated not at all in life. Unmourned in death. Bury his shit in the deep dark and let the worms crawl as they may. Hit it Jesus!

JESUS starts to party, when she is interrupted by SANDY.

SANDY *(standing, loud)*: Sorry, change of plans.

LOLA: What?

SANDY: I'm keeping him. I don't want to bury him. He doesn't deserve it.

A murmur from the church.

He gave all this money to the church so his sins would be forgiven. I'm not forgiving him. And neither should you. He needs to take responsibility!

LOLA: But Nena can't transition until he's gone.

SANDY: Nena?

LOLA: She's stuck on this plane. With me.

SANDY: Where is she? Why can't I see her?

JESUS: You don't have unresolved carajo with each other.

SANDY: Why do I get the shit ghost?

LOLA: You're the one who captured him!

SANDY: Why do you always get everything you want and I'm left cleaning up the crumbs? I want Nena! You take Saúl! He's the one you're so passionate about. I want NENA.

LOLA: I didn't choose–

SANDY: BULLSHIT. You did. You make the rules of this world and you gave me the harder task!

LOLA: You're stronger!

BRUNO: Hey, ladies–

LOLA & SANDY: Shut up!

They drop the tin.

BRUNO: Damn!/

LOLA: You gotta bury him!

SANDY: I dealt with him. I get to do what I want with him!

The church is trembling and there is a feedback loop of sound, sea, Madonna, rage. Like the end of Sgt. Pepper's.

LOLA: Sandy. Let Nena rest–/

JESUS: It's not her who isn't letting Nena rest–/

SANDY *(mad)*: I want to be the rebel! I'm keeping him!/

She shakes the cookie tin.

LOLA *(to Jesus)*: –What do you mean? Nena–!!/

JESUS: You blame Nena. She loves you more than she ever loved herself. She's still trying to make things right.

LOLA: No. I want her to be free!/

SANDY *(getting madder)*: I'm not a secondary character in your story–/

JESUS: You've always blamed her./

LOLA *(to both Jesus and Sandy)*: But it's not that complicated–!/

JESUS: I mean who is the villain here, Lola?/

LOLA: That's not fair!! Don't make me decide! I'm dying!!

SANDY *(mocking)*: I'm dying!

LOLA starts to lose consciousness.

BRUNO *(on his phone!)*: Hello to all the people watching! Hi!!! –My family is batshit cray-cray bunnies!!

LOLA *(dramatic as hell)*: Nena. I'm sorry. Go! Go! And don't wait for me, I'll find my way to you, I'll see you in the next life–

The lights get brighter, the sound louder. JESUS starts to sing.

JESUS *(singing: Like a Virgin)*: "I made it through the wilderness. Somehow I made it Throo-oo-ough–"

LOLA *(fanning herself)*: I don't feel so good.

The church rumbles. LOLA starts to fall. Perhaps she has a seizure, but it is obvious she is in distress.

SANDY: Oh, my god. Lola!

(To Bruno)

Turn that off! Disculpe!

SANDY (CONT'D) *(to the crowd)*: Llamen a una ambulancia—!

BRUNO: Damn—!

LOLA *(real and sincere)*: Nena, take me with you.

LOLA faints, falls off the altar, hard. The noise and lights immediately stop.

BLACKOUT.

THE EDGE

The last light of the sunset hits the apartment, the sun strong through the window. LOLA is asleep, with the JESUS head on her lap. NENA stands absorbing the light.

NENA: I should've prayed to the sun, like my ancestors.

JESUS: Meh. You humans are so binary.

NENA: Cover me in gold, give me drugs and drown me.

JESUS: Ay'hue madre. That Lola is a bad influence.

NENA: She's dramática. I adore her fight. No se deja. Y mi Sandy, tan brillante. They are breaking the chains with their rage.

(A pause)

I did curse them. Is Lola really dying?

JESUS: Eh. Sí. Aren't we all?

NENA: Can I do anything?

JESUS: Chica. You sacrificed everything you got, you got no more. Let her do this her way. She burns very bright. Too bright.

NENA: I was a quiet votive candle.

JESUS: Your life had meaning.

NENA: If you say so. Can I go now?

JESUS: You know you can. Lola's not your responsibility. None of these locos are! Let them sort themselves out. You wanna come back as a tortoise?

NENA: Yes. Someplace quiet. A sunny beach. With no humans!

JESUS: Good luck with that. Humans are worse than cockroaches.

NENA smiles and fades away.

NENA: Adios, Jesús.

JESUS: Adios, Nena. Welcome to the universe.

And she is gone. SAÚL approaches Jesus.

SAÚL *(timidly)*: Disculpe?

JESUS: Ay Díos YO, wait. Your turn will come.

SAÚL: So, it's the devil?

JESUS: Not my decision to make.

A brilliant light. LOLA wakes. She sees that NENA is gone.

LOLA *(to the sky)*: Back and back and back. Your lives had meaning, grandmothers, sisters, aunts. We danced in your wombs, we lived in your skin. We are a chain of love. I honor everything in you, my ancestors. Whoever you were.

JESUS *(grabs and twirls her)*: Ready?

LOLA *(surprised)*: I am. My head isn't hurting.

JESUS: I have a few tricks left up my sleeve.

They dance. LOLA dies. Maybe.

QUICK BLACKOUT TO:

FALL BACK

The apartment looks normal again. LOLA lies on the couch, with a cold compress on her head. SANDY has got her stethoscope out and is checking Lola's pulse. BRUNO is making a phone call. SAÚL is biting his nails and pacing.

BRUNO *(on phone)*: Yo, Drew. Yah, 's Bruno— You're the only number she has in her phone.

He listens.

Naw, man— She's still on the wagon— I think.

He listens hard.

We didn't know.

He listens.

Jesus, you'd think she'd tell her only family—

Mouths "What the—" at LOLA. She gives him the middle finger. She mouths "Stop it" to BRUNO, mouthing to Lola "Wut!?"

(Back to phone)

D-man. I'm sorry. Do you want me to—?

Listens.

I think she'll be happy to hear that but who the fuck knows. Yeah. Bye.

(To Sandy)

Is she OK?

SANDY: She's— I don't know, Bruno. I don't have a baseline for OK with Lola.

SANDY checks LOLA's eyes. Frowns. Tries to get a better look.

LOLA *(singing: "Like a Virgin")*: "I never knew how lost I was, until I found you—ou—ou."

Smiles at SANDY.

Yo.

SANDY *(annoyed, but concerned)*: Tu, que?

LOLA: Why'd we come back here? I wanted a hotel.

BRUNO: You need a hospital.

LOLA: No. People die in hospitals.

SANDY: Can you stop talking in T.V.? God.

BRUNO *(too loudly)*: How many fingers am I holding up—?

LOLA: Quit it. Is there anything to eat?

BRUNO: There is a ton to eat at Tiá Reyna's.

SANDY: They're having an all-meat party.

BRUNO: And there are empanadas.

LOLA *(getting up)*: Ooh. Let's go.

SANDY: Sit the hell down.

LOLA: I'm starving.

SANDY: You passed out.

LOLA: I did?

BRUNO: I got it all. I put it on my Insta story.

BRUNO shows her the phone. We hear the sound of voices on the video: Lola singing, Bruno laughing and Sandy yelling:

LOLA (V.O.) *(on video, muffled)*: "Goddesses of creation, motherfuckers!

BRUNO (V.O.) *(on video, muffled)*: "Heheheheheheheh–"

LOLA *(laughing)*: Oh shit. Hey, my boobs don't look too bad!

BRUNO: Ha ha! Wait– check this–

SANDY: You're both stupid.

They watch Lola fall off the altar on the phone.

LOLA & BRUNO *(stupid gesture)*: Booster rockets, GO!!

SANDY: Are you guys ever going to grow up?

BRUNO: Not me, man. MMM. I want to embrace my inner child till I die.

LOLA: Why are you guys talking to each other?

SANDY: I'm not sure.

BRUNO: You, duh.

BRUNO: Drew's got a handful of overdue medical bills with your name on them.

LOLA: Oop.

BRUNO: He told me to tell you: "Meet you in that one place in Costa Rica."

LOLA: Really? Sexy!

BRUNO *(grossed out)*: Bleah–

SANDY *(grossed out)*: Gross!

SANDY feels around LOLA's neck, and breasts.

LOLA: Fresh!

SANDY: Dude–

LOLA: Just. Shut up, ok? I'm not doing fucking chemo. It's poison, and it doesn't work.

SANDY: Don't tell me, none of my colleagues would ever touch the stuff.

BRUNO: Chemo?

SANDY does a full check up. She checks LOLA's armpit glands.

LOLA: Yep. And I'm still clean so—

(To Sandy)

Hey—!

It tickles.

SANDY: No painkillers.

LOLA: Seems a little irrelevant to be clean at this point. It hurts a fuck load.

BRUNO: Uh. Lo—

LOLA *(she gestures rudely at her brother's sadness)*: None of THAT face. None of that.

SANDY: Huh. I'm not feeling anything.

LOLA: What are you talking about? The mass in my left breast—

She feels. She feels. The mass isn't there.

But— It was huge—

SANDY: Nope.

LOLA: It's not—

She looks at the CREEPY JESUS. He winks.

SANDY: Well— I mean, let's get you home and do a full work up, OK? Jesus, Lo, get a second opinion before you go off the rails.

LOLA: I— I—

LOLA is at an uncharacteristic loss for words. A pause.

BRUNO *(clueless)*: Ladies. I— I mean, I knew you were both cray, and the cray is intense. Do you mind telling me whatthefuck—

SANDY: You weren't born here, I don't think you have to deal with it.

BRUNO: Oh. Cool. Thank the goddess. What the hell do I know, I'm just a gringo—

He gets up.

I'm going to the party.

SANDY: We'll be there soon.

BRUNO exits.

Hey Lola. What about him?

She gestures at SAÚL, who is pacing restlessly.

LOLA: Ugh. He's still here?

SANDY: Yeah.

She waves hello at him. He frowns.

SANDY (CONT'D) *(to Saúl)*: You should chuck yourself into the Rio Magdalena! Like your ancestors.

SANDY takes the vial of blood out on a chain around her neck. Hesitates but puts it in the tin.

(To Lola)

Let's just leave him here. He can be food for the ratones.

LOLA: Oh, that's nice. Poetic. Primitive—

SANDY: Maybe in his next life he won't be such a tool. I wish I had seen Nena.

LOLA: Nena knew you loved her.

SANDY: ...Lo. You're gonna live a long time. You're going to do great things—

LOLA: I know. I'm going to meet Drew in Costa Rica. Last time we were there we had sex in a lot of public places. Shocked the local iguanas.

SANDY: Why are both of you sex fiends?

LOLA: I'm starving.

SANDY: You're always starving.

LOLA: I thought it was the cancer.

SANDY: Nah— it's probably early menopause—

LOLA shushes SANDY.

LOLA: Shhhh— No!

(A beat)

Let's go before Bruno eats all the empanadas.

LOLA gets up. She breathes easy. She searches her pockets.

Who's got the key?

SANDY: I do. I'm giving it to Tere.

LOLA: She deserves it.

SANDY: Yeah. She does.

LOLA: Sand—

SANDY: Ugh. Please don't say anything goopy or hug me.

LOLA: I lov—

SANDY: Stop it. Go. I'll be right there.

LOLA turns to exit, runs back and blows SANDY a kiss. Exits. Sandy stands. To SAÚL:

(Speaking to Saúl)

Your whole life you've been terrified. Now, you have to be brave, Saúl. Braver than you ever thought possible. Wash away your sins in the river. Ask your gods to forgive you. Or go to the devil. Deal with the consequences of how you lived your life. You're not going to get a woman to save you now.

SANDY exits the apartment. CREEPY JESUS smiles at SAÚL then exits, heading to the party. Saúl waits, the tin in his hands. The apartment glows.

BLACKOUT/FIN

Ghosts of Bogotá

PROP LIST

- Hermés Birkin Bag (reasonable facsimile)
- 2 Rolling suitcases
- 3 iPhones Old fashioned key
- JESUS HEAD! (see following page)
- toilet paper
- doll
- cozy
- book
- paper dolls
- broom
- Juan Valdez coffee tray w/ 3 cups
- Bogotá tourist map
- Tray of lasagna
- Two empty (dirty) plates
- Tin cookie box
- Purse for Teresa
- Aguardiente, airplane sized bottle
- bag of empanadas
- laptop for Bruno
- headphones
- multitool
- old fashioned suitcase
- pictures, memorabilia, medals, passports, Anna Karenina in Spanish
- wrapped revolver
- more paper dolls in suitcase, wedding veil or tulle
- bottle of wine
- small ditty bag with vials/envelopes of DNA
- scissors

Scene Breakdown, Props, Costume and Sound/Simple Light plot:
https://docs.google.com/spreadsheets/d/15dGumJNp4IE7uzSiridSOzvPFHicwcgLW_xn_bGIsck/edit#gid=0

Ghosts of Bogotá

"JESUS HEAD" PROP

Below is a reference for the Creepy Jesus Head, referenced in the General Notes at the front of the script:

ABOUT STAGE RIGHTS

Based in Los Angeles and founded in 2000, Stage Rights is one of the foremost independent theatrical publishers in the United States, providing stage performance rights for a wide range of plays and musicals to theater companies, schools, and other producing organizations across the country and internationally. As a licensing agent, Stage Rights is committed to providing each producer the tools they need for financial and artistic success. Stage Rights is dedicated to the future of live theatre, offering special programs that champion new theatrical works.

To view all of our current plays and musicals, visit:

www.stagerights.com

Made in the USA
Las Vegas, NV
03 September 2024